CHARLES FAUDREE
Home

CHARLES FAUDREE *Home*

Charles Faudree
with Francesanne Tucker
Photography by Jenifer Jordan

First Edition
16 15 14 13 12   8 7 6 5 4 3 2 1

Published by
Gibbs Smith
P.O. Box 667
Layton, Utah 84041

1.800.835.4993 orders
www.gibbs-smith.com

Cover and Book Design by Michelle Farinella Design

Printed and bound in China

Gibbs Smith books are printed on either recycled, 100% post-consumer waste, FSC-certified papers or on paper produced from sustainable PEFC-certified forest/controlled wood source. Learn more at www.pefc.org.

Library of Congress Cataloging-in-Publication Data

Faudree, Charles.
Charles Faudree home / Charles Faudree with Francesanne Tucker ; photography by Jenifer Jordan. — First Edition.
pages cm
ISBN 978-1-4236-2122-5
1. Faudree, Charles—Themes, motives. 2. Interior decoration—United States. I. Tucker, Francesanne. II. Title.
NK2004.3.F38A4 2012
747—dc23

2012004657

I dedicate this book to Nicholas, my loving companion for fifteen years.

Contents

On Homes

I SHOULD LEARN NEVER TO SAY NEVER. Over the last few years, I moved into a smaller Tulsa house and sold my second home. I was going to simplify my life. But then I found a wonderful new Tulsa house and a second home in Cashiers, North Carolina, that I simply couldn't resist. I've started all over again.

My life as an author has taken the same path. My last book, *Details,* was to be the last. Then I designed more homes. They were so beautiful and exceptional and I learned so much in the process that I found myself thinking, Why, these rooms need to be published! And so, this book.

Charles Faudree Home gives me the opportunity to share more of my designs and explore in detail what I've learned through the years about the ingredients of a home and its place in our lives. What is home? What makes it special? What makes it truly yours? These are the questions that make my life so interesting. Everyone has a different definition, and as a decorator it's my job to help people find their perfect answer.

Over the years there has been a shift in the basic requirements for a home. Twenty years ago people wanted a good bar; now they want security and a simpler lifestyle. Transitional style with its pared-down design is a response to this change in preference. I respond to the idea of paring down, too, but I like my simpler life to include my favorite collections and a great mix of fabric and furniture.

On a practical level, individual needs vary widely, and those needs have to be fulfilled by the home's design. People use their rooms differently. Some people want to be able to eat in every room in the house. Some want to do jigsaw puzzles in a certain room and some want a piano. A lady with a spectacular collection of scarves must have a closet that is designed to accommodate them.

The trick is to satisfy these everyday concerns while creating an environment that is an expression of the people who live there. We've all known someone who seems ill at ease in their own skin. Unfortunately the same situation can exist with people and their homes. The design of a house can be an awkward fit for its owners. It has to complement them and their lives or, no matter how polished and coordinated, it is a failure.

The single most important ingredient in a home is that it must have a soul. I might wind up in a single room one day, but it will be mine; it will represent me. My friend Miss Pam says my home is made up of playful arrangements of beautiful things that make my guests happy. It is a good description of what I want my home to be.

I am a big believer that a home should have humor and not give you the feeling of being wound up too tight. It should reflect your whole life. It will change because your life is changing. In *Charles Faudree Home* I'll show you how different designs can work to add convenience and beauty to every part of your home.

I am privileged to have friends—designers, artists, family and clients—who have the knack of creating wonderful homes in whatever space they happen to occupy. I have asked a few of them to introduce the sections that follow to add their unique insights on how to make the most of the rooms we live in. I hope you'll enjoy and be inspired by what you see and our observations about home.

Entry and Hallway Design

by **FRANCIE FAUDREE**

THE ENTRY IS MY FAVORITE DESIGN SPACE, *the most frequented and observed of all the public spaces in a home. It is the first and last place your guests see and the area they linger in the longest. A visually stunning entry not only welcomes and wows your guests; it defines your aesthetic as an individual.*

May I offer some suggestions?

Make it beautiful and warm.

Don't make it bizarre or shocking.

Offer your best, but not in a pretentious manner.

Use original art that speaks to you personally.

Don't make it a dark place unless it is a tiny, jewel-box space.

Your entry says hello in your best-dressed way and good-bye in a memorable way as well. First impressions are lasting.

I like to tell people that I taught Charles everything he knows about decorating—I am his sister—but in reality, my suggestions for designing entry halls come with the advantage of years spent watching Charles work his decorating magic.

The entry in my home is an example of his core design principles as my husband, Dale, and I have interpreted them. A fine antique French commode—Charles's favorite entry hall furnishing—holds two French oil lamps that contribute the symmetry of pairs and a large painting by Zoun that reflects our taste in art. A Swedish sofa offers temporary seating, a nearby end table is available to hold a package or purse, and a giltwood mirror is handy for checking lipstick.

Undoubtedly the standout piece in our entry, a sixteenth-century carved wooden blackamoor reflects Charles's taste, because for twenty years it belonged to him. Every time we visited my brother, Dale ask him to "Put my name on this piece . . . just in case you go first." Charles is a kind and generous man. He relinquished the coveted blackamoor to Dale on his sixtieth birthday. The gift illustrated another of my brother's design credos: One of the best ways to enjoy your design treasures is to share them with others.

Previous overleaf: Personal items add flavor to decorating. In Darwin and Linda James' home, I used the owners' riding boots beneath a painting of hunting boots to create a wallscape that draws the eye to the end of the hallway. An antique French horse head from a butcher's shop enhances the equestrian theme.

Facing: Hallways can be more than bypasses used to avoid tramping through every room in the house. They can be functional as well as beautiful, offering temporary resting places for packages, purses and even people. This long hallway gave me the opportunity to include two iron consoles and a chair in addition to the bracketed painting wallscape. A lovely antique French clock defines the far wall.

A landing in Darwin and Linda James' home has the charm of a small room. The French commode holds a custom pewter lamp that adds warmth as well as lighting to the setting.

The indoor use of an antique garden figure adds a touch of whimsy to the entry. The stag resting on top of a French baker's table and the twig mirror reflecting it underscore the woodsy setting of Mark and Cassie Shires' country home.

Facing: I love using different elements in my designs. In Jeff and Sheryl Bashaw's entry I used a simple wine-tasting table to contrast with the formal French elegance of the staircase and chandelier. Art from different periods adds to the mix.

CLASSIC DESIGN STYLES
STOKELY WEBSTER AND HIS PARIS

My sister, Francie, said in the introduction to this section that your entry " . . . not only welcomes and wows your guests; it defines your design aesthetic as an individual." The James entry is a good illustration. It reveals owners with elegant style and a partiality to all things French. And there is definitely a "wow" factor to this formal greeting area. A Regence fruitwood commode anchors the space and is flanked by a pair of Régence fauteuil oreilles, *or wing chairs.*

A Louis XVI garniture ormolu mantel clock with coordinating candelabra is a rare find that makes an impressive display in a formal entry.

Commodes are my favorite entry furnishings. The distressed finish of the Dennis and Leen commode in Steve and Gayle Allen's entry blends with the staircase paneling to create a subtle backdrop for a stone sculpture and onyx-and-crystal hurricane vases.

Above: A formal French entry that is faithful in every detail is lighted by a Belle Époch ormolu and crystal lustre chandelier.

My entry is an expression of my love of all things French, especially Country French antiques. A French Régence bow-front commode holds an impressive terra-cotta pot au feu, *or pot with light, reflected in an 18th-century trumeau mirror. The flanking brackets hold rare tole figures that seem to celebrate a happy country life.*

A generous farm table allowed me to display a variety of interesting accessories in Stewart and Kate Beal's entry hall. Kate is the owner of an antique and gift store, and I wanted to create a welcoming entry hall that reflected her enthusiasm for collecting. A Louis XVI slipper chair introduces the soft color palette used throughout the home

Above: A statue of Joan of Arc celebrating the heroine of the Hundred Years' War is one of many ornaments in the home with a French background. The entry tablescape also includes porcelain flowers by Pamela Tidwell.

A French painted commode by Niermann Weeks is flanked by Louis XVI side chairs in the entry hall. Completing the setting, a hydrangea bouquet and porcelain foxgloves add floral emphasis to the pastoral painting of an antique trumeau mirror.

Facing: The entry I designed for the Cashiers 2011 Designer Showhouse gave me the opportunity to layer wonderful old cabin architecture with European antiques. Double doors open toward a Swedish commode flanked by Louis XVI provincial side chairs and topped with a marvelous Mettlach bowl of apples. The bulls-eye mirror is my own, a treasure piece I found on one of my early trips to England.

Lila and Woolsey, perched on a bench from the Charles Faudree Collection for Thayer Furniture, wait for a walk in Stewart and Kate Beal's entry hall.

An antique garden table adds contrast to more luxurious French furnishings and links the garden terrace that introduces the entry I designed for the Cashiers 2011 Showhouse. An antique birdcage used as wall decor also serves to conceal a kitchen pass through.

The light scale of an antique Swedish sofa is a perfect fit for the small confines of an upstairs landing. I finished the space with crystal lamps, a wallscape centered on a charming framed pattern painting of an Aubusson rug, and a fauteuil chair covered in "Pablo" by Décor de Paris.

The chink and log construction of the Cashiers 2011 Designer Showhouse was a perfect foil for my entry hall design, including Louis XV, Louis XVI and Directoire chairs. The walls were also a great contrast to the antique French wallpaper I framed as artwork. A Lucite table and an Oushak rug add interest to the setting.

An antique trophy cup used as a pencil holder offers a small example of the pleasing results you can achieve from repurposing accessories. Although it is what it seems, a silver dog inkwell adds more charm to the desktop arrangement in the entry hall.

Facing: Covered in "Jute Herringbone" by Greff, an English daybed provides convenient entry hall seating layered with a rich variety of pillows. Above it, an antique American Primitive painting of a young girl highlights pecky cypress paneling.

Francie says, "If something doesn't fit, force it." She's joking, of course, but there is often a way to get around limited space. I wanted seating in a narrow upstairs hallway, and while there weren't many options, I was able to fit diminutive French side chairs whose lack of heft is more than made up for by the striking "Cavallo" fabric by Nancy Corzine that covers them. A collection of hand-colored bird engravings surrounding a Directoire trumeau mirror completes the setting.

A wonderful antique tole jardinière filled with mountain greenery greets visitors in this Cashiers entry. Rare carved dolphin candlesticks made into lamps mounted on Lucite and finished with Fortuny shades complete the tablescape.

Furnishings used in pairs add elegance to a room. The Régence mirror and unusual pearwood cupboard shown here are each one of a pair I used to flank a formal French entry. The bouquet is also repeated to complete the room's harmony. The fauteuil chair I found in France is covered in a gorgeous Fortuny fabric.

A charming entry filled with seaside accessories expresses a Kansas couple's affection for their Cape Cod home. Bracketed coral, a shell-frame mirror, and antique prints of shells welcome visitors to a summer haven by the sea. An outdoor garden trellis worthy of indoor status makes a strong architectural statement in the corner.

All sorts of outdoor furnishings can make great contributions indoors. I use garden seats for cocktail tables on any number of occasions when space is at a premium. The garden seat in this entry is useful but isn't an obstacle for guests to circumnavigate. The bright color is a cheerful bonus in front of a sofa covered in "Island Coral" by Thibaut with custom pillows in "Coralli" by Dedar.

PARIS SECRETS
JED JOHNSON: OPULENT RESTRAINT

Living Rooms

by LISA NEWSOM

I DECORATED MY FIRST LIVING *room when I was five years old. My one-room playhouse was filled with my treasures and the castoffs from our house. My brothers and sisters assisted me with moving furniture around, and then I would reward them with Kool-Aid. Even Kitty, my cat, was invited to celebrate the room's new look. As co-founder of* Southern Accents *and founder of* Veranda, *I have looked at many living rooms since. My view of what makes a successful one remains: make it comfortable and fill it with the things you love.*

Charles Faudree, a friend and colleague for most of my magazine career, understands this, and his love for Country French has greatly inspired me and countless other Francophiles. As an astute designer he enriches the Gallic genre by adding other influences, so that his living rooms, for instance, reflect a perfect combination that makes his style and design classic. Always inviting, these spaces are filled with great antiques, beautiful fabrics and colors, comfortable sofas and chairs that have tables within easy reach and personal collections that are irresistible to the eye and soul of the people who live there.

One interior that immediately comes to mind is a historic residence that he refreshed with dazzling effect on the island of Jamaica. The home, with its loggias and Palladian arches, is more like an Italian villa than a traditional Jamaican house; yet it has the spacious rooms, indoor-outdoor pavilions and tall, conical, wood-beamed roofs typical of the island. For color cues, Charles was inspired by the tropical waters of Montego Bay, seen from the villa's high vantage point. He enlivened the living room with patterned, solid, striped and ikat fabrics on classic and contemporary chairs, sofas and ottomans—all in beguiling shades of bright marine blue. He incorporated blue-and-white porcelains, crystal column lamps, glazed Chinese stoneware lamps, a French-style child's chair and a Dutch painting of peacocks and exotic fowl. White flowers and maidenhair ferns reference the lush flora on the grounds of the estate. For his signature stroke of whimsy, Charles added a touch of coral as the decorative motif on a sofa pillow and, on a side table, a singular oceanic specimen as an objet d'art. The living room is a tour de force of his inimitable style. While many may try to imitate the distinctive Faudree look, few attain his serene results.

Living rooms for far too long were very formal and reserved strictly for guests. But as our lives have become more casual, the living room has become more personal and, best of all, practical. We no longer need or want a room that is seldom used. A living room should be just that: a place for living, an active place for visiting with friends and family, and a quiet retreat for reflection and relaxation.

Congratulations, Charles, on this your sixth book. I have loved each one. Please continue to delight and educate us with your great talent and kind heart.

Charles Faudree's Country French Living
Charles Faudree Interiors
DAVID EASTON Timeless Elegance

Previous overleaf: I keep talking about the value of contrast, and the antique English chinoiserie secretary offers a good visual explanation. The lovely piece would be an asset anywhere, but against rustic old paneling in the living room of a family lodge in the Smokies it becomes a special point of interest. A French bench covered in tiger velvet adds an exclamation point.

Facing: An impressive overmantel is a natural focal point in George Fadaol's living room, accessorized with a pair of antique Staffordshire deer vases and an English bull's-eye mirror. The rare and beautiful majolica cachepot on the coffee table is a prized gift from a friend.

A collection of dog figures gathered around a Staffordshire lamp adds interest to a cozy conversational corner in George Fadaol's living room. The vertical wallscape of hunting trophies and a dog painting adds height to the setting.

Large rooms can stand up to intense colors. In Darwin and Linda James's living room, rich red fabrics embellish upholstered pieces without overwhelming them, as there is space to allow each piece to stand out. A soaring French limestone overmantel leads the eye upward, underscoring the ceiling's height. "Rajah" fabric by Cowtan and Tout is a dramatic departure from the French Louis XVI–style bergère chairs it covers (far right). It adds an exclamation point to a grouping of a French Régence–period commode and antique French paintings.

I love French furnishings, but I wouldn't dream of using them exclusively. The Jameses' living room has many French elements, but Italian altar sticks, an English tea caddy and a contemporary crystal votive add an interesting mix.

Charles Faudree's Country French
Charles Faudree's French Country
FRENCH INTERIORS
THE ART

Facing: When you collect antiques, wonderful stories often come along with them, as is the case with the tole urn I found in the English Cotswolds. It always reminds me of the sweet, elderly lady who owned it. She really hated to sell, she confessed, because "it's been such a good place to hide my gin." In her honor I've turned it into a drinks table between two bergère chairs in my living room.

My goal for my living room was to create the impression of a grand French salon, a formal entertaining area with classic balance and symmetry. The planning for the room required precision and attention to detail in order to define spaces within space, where I could offer hospitality to one person or a whole crowd, while at the same time facilitating easy movement from one area to another. The central location of a Louis XVI daybed makes it work. This wonderful piece directs traffic. It also links its occupants to two separate seating areas as it visually divides the spaces. The round window I added allows light while contributing decorative interest from a wrought-iron grille that was once part of an antique fence. A rococo console by Dennis and Leen occupies the space below the window.

Even though I limited its use, "Le Marchand D'etoffes" by Pierre Frey is the pivotal fabric for my living room. It covers cushions and a single bergère chair that, along with my friend Nicholas, accents the sofa.

To delineate the living area of the open design of Frank and Gayle Eby's Cashiers retreat, I created a large conversation grouping beneath a central chandelier. A wonderful pair of Black Forest plaques frames a second-floor landing overlooking the space.

In Jeffrey and Lisa Rowsey's living room, one large or two separate conversation areas center around a cut-stone mantel by Jim Kelly. Selecting harmonizing soft colors allowed me to use a variety of patterns for the draperies, upholstery and carpeting in this inviting room. Objets d'virtu *is a collection of fine art objects, particularly antiques. It is a good description of the very nice silver collection displayed on the coffee table. Behind it, a provincial-style sofa is sophisticated in silk upholstery.*

I love armchairs. They show off upholstery to advantage, they can be very comfortable, and by introducing more than one style, you can use as many as you want in a single room. Stewart and Kate Beal's living room is an elegant marriage of painted formal and Country French furnishings, with an emphasis on armchairs. A pair of "Patrice" chairs from the Charles Faudree Collection for Thayer Furniture flank a linen-covered Louis XVI sofa, while a graceful fauteuil chair provides a small accent. The large Minton Spidell chairs are not properly armchairs, but their wonderful lines and generous size make them welcome additions to the room.

Against a neutral background, a brightly hued contemporary painting becomes the focal point of Susie Collins' living room, drawing the eye upward and emphasizing the area's generous dimensions. Traditional furnishings, including antique candelabra and bergère chairs covered in "Yasmin" by Lee Jofa, create a good mix with the contemporary touches provided by sisal carpeting and the painting.

Swedish Gustavian chairs with spare architectural lines make good companions to the uncomplicated design of the Lucite table. The "Ocelot" fabric by Cowtan and Tout adds interest to the sleek arrangement.

An English painting of man and his best friend is appropriately placed above the green toile living room chair that is a favorite napping spot for George Fadaol's dog, Mr. Green.

I played up a nice 19th-century Dutch pine armoire by surrounding it with a collection of blue delft jars and plaques. A rare rafraichissoir, *or wine and cheese table, now serves as a tea table.*

The use of pairs can create an elegant space, whatever the style. A pair of carved antique panels emphasizes the height of floor-to-ceiling windows in Cindy and David Foster's living room. Other pairs of sofas and chairs upholstered in neutral fabrics create a stylish palette for the room. An ottoman paired with two smaller leather-covered footstools adds a pleasing departure from the identical matching pairs scheme.

In Steve and Gayle Allen's living room, a Louis XV–style mirror reflects a harmoniously balanced seating arrangement centered around a Lucite coffee table by Alan Knight. I used Billy Baldwin–inspired slipper chairs to add another contemporary ingredient to the setting.

There are easy ways to call attention to special furnishings. In this example I created an eye-catching still life by stacking books and a pair of glasses on a beautifully carved chair.

Below: A convex buffet deux corps *by Dennis and Leen is a towering piece that dominates the corner of the living room. In front of it I placed a Lucite table with Napoleon III–style side chairs to create an attractive mix.*

Blue-and-white fabrics and accessories establish a color scheme that creates a cool garden room haven. A Swedish porcelain stove adds sculptural interest to the corner of the room. "Avril" fabric from the Charles Faudree Collection for Vervain, depicting baskets, watering cans and flowers, was a natural choice for this room, and I used it extensively for curtains and as upholstery for a Louis XVI–style chair.

Essential MONET

Previous overleaf: Historically, one of the main uses for mirrors was to reflect and brighten a room lit by candlelight. The large mirrors in Jeff and Sheryl Bashaw's living room do add brightness, but their main contribution is the regal formality of their Louis XV–style giltwood framing. Armchairs beneath them are covered in "Mondeville" from the Charles Faudree Collection for Vervain. Sadie sits on one of a pair of solid-covered sofas that are made more interesting because they are not identical.

Facing: Swedish furniture is usually painted, giving it a mellow patina that warms many different decorating styles. The antique Swedish pine secretary in the Shires' country home is a natural companion to stone walls and bleached wood flooring.

Curtains in "Biron Check" from the Charles Faudree collection for Vervain mix with formal furnishings to establish a casual atmosphere in a country home living room. A custom stag lamp and a majolica tree trunk table add to the woodsy feel of the room. Gigi, the mistress of the home, accents a Swedish-style sofa.

A gorgeous velvet pillow in "Sang Sacre" by Sabina Braxton repeats the color of a classically styled commode from Aix en Provence.

A Louis XVI armoire, c. 1760, is topped with an antique tole tray and a celadon vase that repeats the blue hues that accent the room. The fauteuil chair is covered in "Kessier Damask" by Travers.

At the Kappa Alpha Theta house I used "Cottage Rose" fabric by Stroheim and Romann for curtains and chairs in the living room. It is a cheerful, casual fabric that banishes any feeling of austerity from the very large space. Grouping a number of chairs in a large semicircle provides a comfortable setting for relaxing and sharing friendship during busy days.

Previous overleaf: When Frank and Gayle Eby purchased the 2010 Cashiers Showhouse in North Carolina, my first task was to "give some age" to the home's fairly new construction. Tulsa wood craftsman David Hollingsworth amended the architecture to include old-wood paneling and beams that add warmth to the living room and the kitchen and dining room beyond. The marvelous retreat features a rich mix of antiques that share a rural heritage and a liberal supply of comfortable upholstered pieces.

A Venetian mirror, an 18th-century French commode and an antique Black Forest deer add international charm to the corner of a living room. The eye-catching child's armchair that completes the setting is covered in "Tigertooth" by Jane Shelton.

Layering fabrics was key to the inviting seating area in Frank and Gayle Eby's home in the Smoky Mountains. The signature fabric, "Vanderlyn Crewel" by Ralph Lauren, covers imposing porter chairs separated by a leopard-print bench in front of the fireplace. Four contoured club chairs are upholstered in "Mondeville" from the Charles Faudree Collection for Vervain. And the sofa, upholstered in "Nicholas" from the Faudree Collection, holds a variety of pillows in rich contrasting fabrics and textures. The prominent painting above the mantel is from the owners' Jamaica home.

I love the symmetry of Stephen and Gaye Sherman's living room. A pair of sofas covered in "Kid Mohair" by Beacon Hill is accompanied by a pair of gold leaf chairs from Michael Taylor upholstered in "Coral Velvet" by Nancy Corzine. Pairs of lamps, tables, mirrors and even plants complete the elegant design. The very formality of the room makes the introduction of an abstract painting by Greg Gummersall all the more interesting.

Comfortable seating should never be the victim of great style. A sofa covered in "Soligny Chenille" by Brunschwig and Fils is joined by a daybed filled with luxurious pillows, a settee upholstered in "Mirabeau" from the Charles Faudree Collection for Vervain and a roomy toile bench. Porcelain brackets hold carved wooden urns on either side of a lovely French tapestry that is the focal point of the room.

Seashell engravings, pillows covered in fabric with a coral motif and a seashell obelisk are some of the marine accessories I used in James and Julie Welch's beach house. However, it was actually the wonderful antique Swedish secretary, with no relationship to the ocean at all, that was the starting point for the home's interior design. The sculpture on the coffee table is by Julie Welch.

Regardless of the color scheme, I love a painted blue ceiling. Traditionally used for porches, a blue ceiling works wonders indoors, adding an outdoor, breezy feel to a room. For the cottage living room I limited the entire color scheme to blue plus white, creating an airy atmosphere that enlarges its apparent space. The white painted mantel is by Young and Fancy Signs.

Libraries and Clubrooms

by DAVID EASTON

I CONFESS I HAVE AN ADDICTION *to books. I must have four to five thousand of them, and counting. My office, apartment and house are filled to the max and I have still more books in storage. It is a sickness, but since I have a decorating and architecture office, I can justify them, and they are part of what makes my life fun.*

In my libraries I like having all the shelves on the same line because staggered shelving makes my eyes jumpy. I love having picture lights above the shelves; it gives much-needed light and creates a wonderful play of light and shadow. In our house in the country, we have a rolling ladder attached to the shelves so all the books are accessible. It is sculptural and practical as well.

In addition to their own worth, books do a lot of decorating. Old books add the same patina to a room as do good antiques. I also like the look of a few objects mixed in on the shelves. Even a nice small painting hung over a bookshelf adds a wonderful layered look to a library.

I have known Charles for thirty-odd years and have seen the various libraries he has designed. They may be pine-paneled or painted, but all of them display books in a most attractive way. He always includes wonderful objects on the shelves and pictures here and there. He creates rooms that function, and does so beautifully.

Whether library or clubroom, Charles always incorporates comfortable sofas and furnishings and the odd pieces that make any room a delight. Our decorating philosophy is the same: approach any room with the goal of making it the most attractive and comfortable, the room you want to live in the most.

BORDEAUX CHAT

Previous overleaf: In John And Julie Nickel's clubroom I used pairs of elements—beginning with bergère chairs covered in the "Tree of Life" pattern by Lee Jofa—to create the elegance in keeping with the room. The focal point of the accessory pairs is a large painting that does double duty as a work of art and a decorative disguise for a television. The television is indispensable to the way we live now, but in situations where it would create a false note I like to conceal it with a hinged painting or an armoire. Some of the newer technologies include paintings that actually roll up and TVs that appear to be mirrors when not in use.

Facing: The theme for the Nickels' clubroom began at the Paris flea market when Julie discovered four wonderful needlepoint-covered chairs. They are partnered with an English Regency mahogany and lemonwood pedestal table.

Comfort is essential to good design. That's what inviting rooms are all about. But there's a common misconception that elegant rooms can't be easy to live in. This clubroom illustrates that antiques and treasures can add to the pleasure of a room designed for casual entertaining. Even the pool table is a refined piece custom built to blend with its surroundings.

A French daybed covered in natural linen is piled with pillows for comfortable seating in a library that also serves as a music room. The Louis XVI fauteuil chair is covered in "Kessier Damask" by Travers.

Facing: Over an Italian library table, I used antique Audubon engravings to create the background for a striking 1860s English bronze figure. Pastel-colored lampshades and pillow fabric add a light touch to the clubroom.

Pale antique pine paneling provides good contrast for an exceptional pair of bronze doré candelabra and a dark marble mantel in Darwin and Linda James's library.

A handsome bronze steer-horn vase accessorizes the library coffee table.

Warm fabric colors and mellow antique pine paneling invite solitary readers or whole troops of guests to enjoy the library. I used lighted wall sconces mounted on the sides of the bookcases to emphasize the intimate recess they create.

In Frank and Gayle Eby's clubroom, a planked wood ceiling and stone walls provide the perfect backdrop for a mix of animal print fabrics and "Fleur Exotique" from the Charles Faudree Collection for Vervain. The theme creates an aura of far-flung adventure, reflecting the owners' many travels.

Arches are a unifying theme in Steve and Gayle Allen's library, used in the bookcase design and repeated in the doors of the handsome Minton-Spidell secretary. Warm colors and rich fabrics create a room that is both stylish and inviting.

While the use of color is restrained in Susie Collins's clubroom, the effect is a bright, happy reflection of its owner. The stone dove on the mantel attracts attention precisely because it is not one of a pair, and directs the eye to the antique French barometer above.

Facing above: Perhaps it's not quite like sitting under a tree reading a book, but the plump sofa beneath a pastoral painting offers a serene spot for reading in Frank and Gayle Eby's well-stocked library. Majolica plates on antique Black Forest brackets and miniature artworks flank the painting.

For a family with three active boys I wanted to establish a polished design that was both comfortable and sturdy. The large seating area includes a pair of "Monique" armchairs from the Charles Faudree Collection for Thayer Furniture flanking an antique French wedding armoire that hides the television. A large ottoman doubles as a coffee table between two club chairs.

Greek jars are displayed in a Regency-style cabinet front, recessed to allow more space in the Allens' clubroom. The Directoire-style chaise by Dennis and Leen reflects the room's neoclassical theme.

Hours spent at your desk with a computer or checkbook can be a little monotonous, so I like to fill these areas with favorite memorabilia. On Linda James's library desk, her love of horses is reflected by a very personal collection of horse figures, engravings, bronzes and an equestrian trophy.

FRENCH FARMHOUSES AND COTTAGES
Paul Walshe • John Miller
THE DECORATIVE CARPET
ALIX G. PERRACHON
CHRIS MADDEN
AT HOME

"Cavalier Toile" from the Charles Faudree Collection for Vervain is a pastoral print including horses—a logical fabric for an equestrian's library.

A farm table used as a sofa-back table holds a pair of custom spelter lamps, an artful display of accessories and, most important, Flipper the goldfish, who is much admired by the Beal family's dog, Lily.

A Dutch painting from Antique Warehouse is a strong decorative element of the clubroom's design. Beneath it, perfectly nice Black Forest lamps have been promoted to outstanding design originals with the addition of custom paisley shades.

I love shopping in Europe for fabulous one-of-a-kind pieces, but increasingly great design is available without airplane tickets, security lines or bad weather delays. The mellow wood construction of a pair of bibliotheques *from Restoration Hardware is perfectly suited to a large clubroom, adding architectural interest to a welcoming collection of upholstered pieces, including club chairs covered in fabric by B. Berger.*

A striking contemporary painting, Magic Circle, *by Joe Andoe, a New York painter and author with Oklahoma roots, commands center stage in the library. Fabrics, including a sofa covered in "Cantaloupe Hide" by Vervain and a club chair covered in "Ishtar" by Vervain, unite with the Shermans' dog, Gabby, to create a warm atmosphere for the room. Books covered in white have a crisp textural appearance that relates to the painting.*

A former kitchen nook has grown into a library for serious readers with the addition of floor-to-ceiling shelving, a desk and Dennis and Leen wing chairs covered in "Pardah Print" by Lee Jofa.

THE BLUE CHAIR JAM COOKBOOK
BREAKFAST
THE HEIRLOOM TOMATO
pig
CHINA
DOGWOODS
EASTERN FOREST
PLENTY

For a home with a blue and white color palette I used a variety of fabric patterns, including "Burnet" by Kravet, a fun fabric covering the French chair in a corner of the library. A small white garden stool serves as a drinks table.

I designed James and Julie Welch's second home on Cape Cod to reflect the sun-filled skies and ocean views that surround it. Fresh white walls and blue-and-white fabrics predominate, and many of the accessories have an aquatic focus. As the home is small, the library is a multipurpose area including a desk, plenty of spots for reading and, of course, that wonderful, wonderful view.

FROMAGE
FORT

Kitchens

by HAL AINSWORTH AND WINTON NOAH (SHARED WITH ALICE SCANLON)

KITCHENS STAND ALONE *as the most inviting room in a house. Certainly that is true at the Ainsworth-Noahs. Theirs is intricately designed so two can dance, so Hal the cook (oven always set at 450 degrees) and Winton the baker (oven barely at 325 degrees), need not share the surfaces nor spar over appliances, just collectively savor the culinary moments. It's cleaner that way and calmer after the hectic workweek, because the hustle and bustle of this kitchen is about the friends parading through it and the panoramic views outside this mountain aerie.*

A big old iron stove sets the mood, complemented by Hal's French cookware. Charles might disagree, though: he'd point rather covetously to the black Chippendale shelf over the stove lovingly laden with blue-and-white willow ware and crystal with honeycomb fretting. But either way, it's never about what's in a kitchen; rather it's all about who's in there, and those are your favorite people.

Memories are the magic formula central to kitchens. Winton's vision is informed by a picture of his grandmother's old (you guessed it) iron stove stacked with iron skillets and of the family gathering for ice cream on the porch behind. Hal recalls the southern smells of fried chicken and peach pies. Each fiercely followed the vibrant voices from those places in creating their own kitchen spaces.

Whether feeding 125 out of their first mountain kitchen—a Pullman 9 x 14—or constantly hosting a whirl of benefits in Cashiers, the parade of folks is always kitchen bound. This Thanksgiving you might have been greeted warmly at the front door by your host, Winton, but you soon would have gravitated with a bevy of others to the smells in their kitchen, and to the commanding presence of Hal.

Splendidly attired in warm fall colors, Charles, too, will have migrated there. The kitchen expands with his presence; the casseroles created from each guest's holiday family favorite foods follow him in, the chopping and carving move faster and the glasses clink more often. The kitchen has become everyone's home away from home.

Charles is a jolly good fellow amongst his friends here: so generous with his time for Cashiers Showhouses, antique fairs and countless book signings. He is also kind in sharing his Tulsa friends and family. Charles and our kitchen are as one; they consistently produce the ultimate in good taste and they ask nothing in return.

Previous overleaf: A simple architectural antique can transform new construction. This fabulous old window was a Paris flea market find that we included in the home's plans from the beginning. The window highlights a bronze antique mistletoe chandelier.

My kitchen accessories are definitely inclusive, ranging from noble portrait plaques to bucolic Staffordshire cows. The carved limestone sink is from Natural Stone Sources.

Facing: Recycling used items from our kitchens is becoming a popular routine, but I like to expand the idea to include recycling old items to *our kitchens as well. In my kitchen I've recycled the end of an antique daybed to cover a necessary, but pretty hideous, vent hood. I also recycled a Regency mirror to decorate the space above the stove as well as to catch grease spatters. The contrast with the contemporary stove adds interest, proving, as I've said—not for the last time—it's all about the mix, not the match.*

FAUROY
Velars près Dijon.
EPSOM SALT

I used a Louis XV–style buffet custom built in France to serve as a center island and covered storage with a pair of salvaged doors, converting an unremarkable kitchen into a gracious room complete with a formal chandelier.

The top of a French cupboard was repurposed as a vent hood and painted to match the rest of the Allen kitchen, while a small Black Forest cow holds center stage.

AMPHORA
EPSOM SALTS

The center island in my kitchen is a converted farm table, which contrasts with a more upscale Belgian buffet deux corps *that adds concealed storage space. Below, my Cavalier, Ruby, is on the alert for dropped treats.*

I used antiques and old wood to add history to the kitchen in Frank and Gayle Eby's Carolina home. Simple open shelving and an antique Swedish cupboard supply "new" old storage, while an antique pewter server made into a custom lamp provides lighting.

Biscotti

In France, architectural salvage treasures are as plentiful as hair ribbons. Countless stores and flea market stalls sell everything from dormers to mantels to staircases to doorknobs. So many beautiful things were made that nothing should be wasted . . . and very little is. Starting with an architectural fragment that may originally have decorated an armoire, I added a pair of Country French doors and applied an antique paint finish. The result is an amazing pantry that will never be duplicated.

A nineteenth-century Staffordshire cow forms the base of a custom lamp that accessorizes a countertop.

Previous overleaf: For a new home I chose French-style tiles custom painted by Janet Davie to complement the owners' wonderful blue-and-white export china. A custom wrought-iron and bronze chandelier by Dale Gillman hangs above a nineteenth-century terra-cotta water filter that is used as an appealing vase for flowers.

Useful items chosen with care for their beauty make an attractive kitchen tablescape.

A French boucherie*, or butcher's shop, traditionally advertised its location with a bull's head above the doorway. This sign is now a delightful wall hanging in the kitchen of the James home.*

VIKING

The fern motif of a custom tole chandelier suggests a garden setting appropriate to the open-air pool house kitchen. The custom vent hood incorporates a reclaimed carved panel.

For a Cape Cod home, I hunted through local shops for accessories with a New England past. One of my favorites is an antique egg poacher I used for a custom lamp. It highlights pewter pieces on an antique jam cupboard—also a local find—and a nice collection of majolica oyster plates.

Faux finishes are at least as interesting as the real thing. Scalamandré's "Quaker Barn Board" wallpaper transforms a kitchen wall into a colorful impression of wood siding. A faux finish also adds to the appeal of a vent hood, giving it the look of old stone construction, which is a nice contrast to the frankly modern cooktop.

Facing: A vent hood covered in old wood and decorated with an antique wood fragment adds a bucolic feel to a kitchen in the mountains. A Black Forest carving is featured above the contemporary stove.

Facing: I used a banquette with a variety of colorful pillows to maximize kitchen seating and added a drop-leaf table that is ideal for a small space. The American candlelight chandelier is an antique that has been electrified.

In a kitchen with room for a seating area that didn't have to double as an eating space, I had the fun of covering furnishings with a mix of fabrics from Kravet without giving a single thought to spilled jam. White curtains and accessories create an unobtrusive background for the playful fabric combinations.

Dining Rooms

by JAMES STEINMEYER

HAVING LIVED IN NEW YORK *for the past thirty-eight years, I have never had the luxury of a dining room, as apartment living usually has only dining space. My first real dining room is in our Tulsa home. I love the idea of it, as you can walk away after a meal and go to another part of the house.*

It has two floor-to-ceiling windows and two antiqued mirrored niches with Italian consoles that I got from Charles. White walls and creamware plates set off white marble floors. A round Biedermeier table with modern chairs always holds candles that are reflected in the mirrors. It is a pretty room, and it is fun to have friends over to share it with.

I guess that is what it is all about, in the end. If you love your friends—and for me cooking is a great way to show my love for them—nothing beats a good dinner or lunch at home. The dining room becomes the stage set for entertaining.

Charles is a serial mover and has had a number of dining rooms in the thirty-some years I've known him. There have been formal ones, less formal ones, small ones and sometimes dining rooms that were just an area at one end of the living room. They have all been different but equally inviting.

As Charles is a great collector, the focal point of his dining room may be the blue-and-white export china that he collects, or a new chandelier he could not live without or some other collection he has developed. No matter how he shuffles his collections, adds new chairs or dresses an old favorite in a new fabric, uses a round table or an oblong one, the one constant is the inviting space he creates for his friends.

Charles has great affection for his friends and loves to share a meal with them. He creates the same kind of wonderful dining spaces for his clients, in individualized variations so they, too, can have a wonderful stage for entertaining.

Previous overleaf: A carved giltwood mirror in the Régence style holds center stage above a commode in George Fadaol's dining room. A pair of custom lamps in the style of Napoleon III flanking the mirror adds stately contrast.

Facing: It's hard to say which is more important to the success of this breakfast room, the warmth of the mellow stone wall or the outstanding majolica collection that decorates it. I used a provincial wall shelf to complete the wallscape and added a petrin, *or dough box, beneath it to complete the cozy French setting.*

An antique Régence commode holds a custom lamp made from a Napoleon III–style spelter figure topped with a striped silk shade. A 19th-century portrait adds a finishing French touch to the dining room setting.

Previous overleaf: Striking "Bazoches" wallpaper by Pierre Frey is layered with luxurious striped drapes to establish the mood for a grand dining room. Checks are approachable and belong everywhere, from ballrooms to country kitchens. Here, "Accent Checks" by Chelsea covers Louis XV–style French chairs and lines a buffet à deux corps *that displays a collection of English stoneware.*

Facing: I used two very different lighting sources to add to the interest of a dining room tablescape. Italian altar sticks contrast with a contemporary onyx lamp to flank a painting above an inherited Italian commode.

My favorite saying, "It's all about the mix, not the match," can be even more important in rooms with subtle differences. In Susie Collins' exceptional dining room there is little variation in fabric colors, but the unexpected mix of leather side chairs and velvet host chairs is much more interesting than a single texture and pattern for seating.

Painted finishes and provincial styles unite French chairs with an Italian table. A charming twig-and-leaf chandelier and simple white pottery displayed on open shelves reinforce the breakfast room's country flavor.

For a transitional dining room, I paired a Lucite table from Alan Knight with Italian chairs from Minton Spidell. An antique buffet from the Paris flea market holds antique altar sticks converted into lamps and a pair of tole bouquets flanking a contemporary vase. The mirror, by Dale Gillman, was originally a French window.

Previous overleaf: Nothing equals the ability of a chandelier with real candles to create a special ambience for an intimate dinner party. Finding such a fixture is a project in itself—this Italian chandelier was a Paris flea market find—but well worth the effort. A Belle Époque mirror reflects the candlelight and discreet ceiling lighting, while decorative lamps add wattage. Curtains and chair upholstery are in "Le Grande Chanticleer" by Schumacher.

The intensity of a single color sets the predominant theme for an elegant Country French dining room.

"Halsey Plaid" fabric by Thibaut is a classic pattern that is a natural addition to a countryside cabin's dining room. Both the tin artisan chandelier and tole footbath support the home's rural identity.

My breakfast area is dominated by a Swedish secretaire *that is an important member of my "old favorites," treasured pieces that have moved with me from house to house over the years, as well as spending time in the homes of friends. A special collection of pottery and porcelain and framed old menus accessorize the space, along with a painting of recumbent cows that has a place of prominence.*

Overleaf: The restrained design of a dining room emphasizes each element. Classic host chairs are covered in modern embroidered linen, "Windermere" by Travers. "Brook Street" fabric by Zoffany on the side chairs is a traditional velvet stripe, but its combination of vivid colors adds a contemporary twist. The fabric combination underscores the room's featured accessory, an abstract painting expressed in the same colors. An antique crystal chandelier that is a family heirloom has a place of prominence in a contemporary dining room.

J. Louis
C. Rosat.
V. Alth.

FRENCH CHATEAU
FRANCE & ITALY

Wonderful marble floors and the symmetry introduced by pairs of chandeliers, wall sconces and decorative plates create an elegant setting for casual dining in the sun room of Bob and Ann Osborne's home. I used cozy Country French furnishings—an antique settee and chairs upholstered in "François" from the Charles Faudree Collection for Vervain, and an iron and parquet table—to contrast with the formal space.

An iron light fixture by Formations casts a soft glow over the dining table in the Ebys' home in Cashiers, North Carolina. Rich neutrals, including dining chairs covered in "Apache" by de Le Cuona and curtains made from "Sarawak Paisley" fabric by Schumacher, blend with antique wood paneling to create a warm, inviting setting for entertaining.

DARMS LANE
DARMS LANE
DARMS LANE
DARMS LANE

Entertaining

by LINDA JAMES

THE JOY OF ENTERTAINING, *or, as the French say,* le plasir d'inviter, *truly is an art form. People love to be invited into your home. Whether it's a formal dinner with many hours of planning or a spontaneous simple gathering, the unexpected pleasure of just being invited is always appreciated. When you open your home to others, in a sense you open your heart.*

We were fortunate enough to envision and build a home combining our tastes, love of antiques, and all things French with Charles's expertise and signature style. We love to entertain and wanted every room to embrace guests with comfort and warmth and to welcome them from the moment they enter.

One of the many things we learned from Charles is that whether your home is filled with priceless treasures or flea market finds, it will be inviting if you give consideration to every single detail. He designed our home to display articles and collections that have woven the tapestry of our lives—our family, our accomplishments, travels and passions. He created a wonderful environment that perfectly suits us, one where our guests feel at ease and comfortable.

I think Charles creates welcoming rooms because he is a welcoming person. Soon after we finished our home, I invited several of my high school friends to join me for lunch, and Charles paid a surprise visit. Upon his arrival, they were all immediately put at ease by his warmth, charm and inimitable grace. Within five minutes, it was as if they had known him for years.

I was in the kitchen preparing lunch and suddenly there was Charles. Without a second thought, he picked up the plates and served each one of my guests as though they were his own. When lunch was finished, he insisted on clearing the table. For someone with such an incredibly demanding schedule to take time for my friends was an honor in itself. For him to help me entertain them was a gift of his time and an example of his generosity.

New acquaintances became old friends around my table. Certainly that day my friends and I were fortunate to have truly experienced le plasir d'inviter. Merci, Monsieur Faudree.

Previous overleaf: An antique French sign in Larry and Carol Bump's wine cellar has been painted by artist Janet Davie to represent Darms Lane, the Bumps' vineyard in Napa Valley. Beneath it, an antique console serves as a tasting table.

I used bronze Louis XVI–style fire irons as unexpected accessories on the bar in the wine room.

Facing: A continental nobleman with a wine-colored cravat looks down on a tray of spirits.

DOLCE

CRICHTON HALL
Chateau Ste Michelle

With their extensive wine collection as a background, Gary and Donna Gilliam's wine cellar is an attractive spot for a wine tasting. A wine barrel serves a table for uncorking.

A cache of corks from past wine tasting experiences is an interesting collection on a ledge.

The muted tones I used for armchairs and leather-covered theater chairs in this entertainment room combine with sound-absorbing green-flannel-covered walls to create a hushed atmosphere perfect for enjoying serious cinema or a really good movie.

The marriage of two Country French pieces creates custom built-in storage in Darwin and Linda James's wine room. A buffet holds the sink, icemaker and storage, and a former dish cupboard now displays wine glasses.

This exceptional wine room is appropriate for John and Julie Nickels, members of one of Napa Valley's leading wine-producing families. Wine making is an art, and in this room we created art by displaying a wine collection behind decorative antique ormolu and wrought-iron doors. Georgian mohair-covered chairs from Dennis and Leen accompany a table appropriate for dining or wine tasting. A magnificent Mettlach hot wine pot, centered on the table, adds a final wine-inspired touch to the room's design.

A Belle Epoch–style buffet in the wine room displays wine and wine-associated accessories. Ruby crystal lamps with claret-colored Fortuny shades, a pair of topiaries in miniature wine buckets and a pair of wine bottles flank a Black Forest clock.

45

A bust of Bacchus, the god of wine, presides over a highly effective wine display built by Tulsan David Hollingsworth.

In an elegant home filled with French antiques, the owners wanted to create an entertainment room that had the opulent feel of an intimate Parisian theater. The gold-leafed faux balcony was a major element, establishing an aura of grandeur while concealing the projector. Red velvet seating trimmed with gold bullion fringe added to the luxurious feel, while more gold leaf on moldings and on the chandelier completed the setting.

Outdoor Spaces

by GAYLE EBY

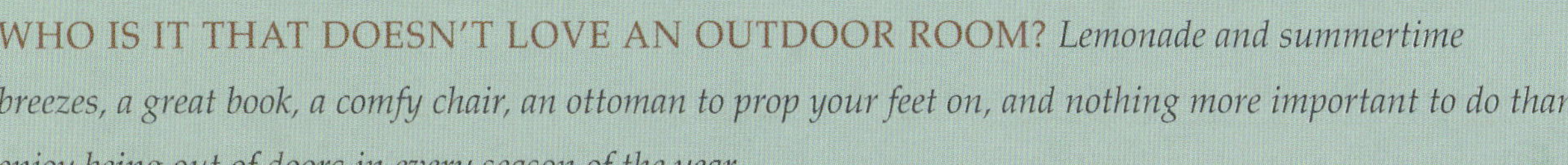

WHO IS IT THAT DOESN'T LOVE AN OUTDOOR ROOM? *Lemonade and summertime breezes, a great book, a comfy chair, an ottoman to prop your feet on, and nothing more important to do than enjoy being out of doors in every season of the year.*

Perhaps because of his upbringing in the wooded landscapes and sunny pastures of eastern Oklahoma, Charles Faudree has a keen appreciation for the wonders of nature and an unerring ability to incorporate that feeling into his interior designs. Charles may use outdoor statuary in an entry hall or put a fauteuil chair meant for an elegant living room on a porch. And he makes it all work.

Much of our enjoyment of our home in Cashiers, where Charles has created designs for our porches that embrace that beauty, comes from the spectacular countryside of the Smoky Mountains. One porch has a roof and a large fireplace that offers warmth and some protection from the uncertain mountain climate. Charles furnished it beautifully: a sofa, upholstered chairs, tables, lamps, accessories and even portieres. It is a marvelous room—indoors or out.

His thoughtful design has given us the opportunity to really live in our landscape. On one memorable evening the weather turned against us just as our guests were arriving for an outdoor evening. We closed the portieres, started a fire in the hearth, lighted candles and had a perfect party. It was simply magical.

Previous overleaf: Homes need to be furnished with their owners' interests in mind. I love puzzles, so the porch of my country home had to include a table for my hobby. My home is also a retreat from my often-frenzied schedule, so a daybed is decorative as well as a perfect place for a snooze accompanied by the splashing sounds of Spring Creek below. Postscript: my restful retreat is now my former home. I have found a better getaway that will be even more relaxing, but it is going to require a lot of work and effort and decorating and is going to keep me very busy for the foreseeable future . . . but that's a story for another time.

The arched entry of a side porch frames an iron chandelier. A pair of striking iron mirrors highlight the porch shell accessories, and iron furnishings reflect the open-air locale.

Overleaf: The decorating possibilities for outdoor living areas have been revolutionized by the improvements in outdoor fabrics. Any design is possible. For this side porch, I created a room complete with upholstered sofas, pillows and chairs. Now the gracious indoor furnishings visible through the open doorway are repeated in this wonderful porch living room.

An unusual antique stone swan steals the scene from its dining table perch on the porch of Mark and Cassie Shires's lake home.

Facing: An old wooden canoe used as a wall hanging reflects the lakeside location of a screened porch.

PARIS

I'm a firm believer that outdoor rooms should be enjoyed as much as possible, and including a TV makes it more likely that people will spend time there. Above a stone mantel in an outdoor living area a wonderful old French military sign—replicated by Tulsa artist Janet Davie—opens to reveal a television. Ample seating includes a pair of "Patrice" wing chairs from the Charles Faudree Collection for Thayer Furniture and a sofa covered in "Samoa Stripe" by Schumacher.

The outdoor room gets extra distinction from a custom chandelier by Dale Gillman and a pair of antique doors I used to frame the French doors leading to the living room. An antique table with a zinc top adds space for casual dining.

Ferns decorating an outdoor fabric set the tone for a pool house. Other foliage—living, painted and sculpted—continues the botanical theme. The painting rolls up to reveal a TV.

A custom seashell box decorates a limestone mantel.

An ivory box and a whimsical tole palm tree complement their setting.

Nothing can compete with the fabulous views from Frank and Gayle Eby's porch overlooking the Smoky Mountains. I used simple furnishings from McKinnon and Harris and accented the sofa with bright pillows that are changed seasonally.

This wonderful terrace is all things French. An antique Country French iron and limestone baker's table serves as a buffet for outdoor dining underneath a French café sign. The large containers holding evergreens are vases d'Anduze, named for the village in Provence where they are made. The mellow backdrop of old stone walls and pavers that pulls the setting together is, unbelievably, new construction.

Iron furniture from Murray's Iron Works provides a comfortable poolside seating area. The chairs are upholstered in outdoor fabric from Stroheim and Romann, while the sofa is upholstered in Silver State fabric.

A formal pool house has as much sophistication as the main home's indoor rooms, including draperies, upholstered pieces and a painting hinged to disguise a television set.

Porches play an important role in Frank and Gayle Eby's Cashiers home. For a screened porch that opens from the dining room, I included drapes to protect it so that the wonderful summer-in-the-mountains weather could be enjoyed with the comfort of indoor furnishings. Painted chairs are upholstered in "Palmier Union" by Cowtan and Tout.

An antler mirror and stone lamps from Formations add indoor luxury to a screened porch.

A lower-level porch provides a great eating space for grandchildren at the Eby retreat. I surrounded a farm table with a collection of sturdy chairs and an antique Country French bench with a cushion covered in "Biron Check" fabric from the Charles Faudree Collection for Vervain.

French furnishings are often thought of as formal, but the French have a countryside, too, and furniture for rural entertaining. These French folding chairs and dining table on my former cabin's porch reflect my love of all things French, even in a very casual setting.

Bedrooms and Bathrooms

by BARRY DIXON

EVEN EXCLUDING THE ROMANTIC POSSIBILITIES, *one could certainly argue that the bedroom is the most important room in a home. It is the alpha and omega of daily existence, and in the best instances the bedroom not only gets our day off to the best possible start but soothes our soul at day's end, allowing the blissful renewal of body and mind that are so important as we repeat the twenty-four-hour cycle.*

And the bathroom! The bath is our most private sanctuary, a sacred realm for connecting body with said soul in total isolation from the outside world and all it represents. The evolution of design has betrothed one to the other in modern interior's happiest marriage.

I've the good fortune of calling Mr. Faudree a friend. We both design fabrics for our wonderful friends at Vervain, whose corporate headquarters happen to be in Tulsa, Oklahoma, Charles's hometown. This fortunate coincidence has allowed me to get to know him better and, lucky for me, to be a guest in his home, where, as you might expect, his talent and warm, gentlemanly hospitality greet you at the door. Nowhere do these qualities shine brighter than in the cozy bedroom suites, where every thoughtful detail has been considered and employed.

I noticed the same quiet attention lavishly layered in the bedrooms and baths of my neighbors' home in Warrenton, Virginia. Of course, Charles had done their home as well. The crisp comfort and soft sensibilities were there, again, ready to receive.

We can all learn from Charles's timelessly gracious approach.

Previous overleaf: Discovering a wonderful antique dressing room mirror led to a search for a base to do it justice. I found it in an antique French console that has been fitted with a sink and used for a powder room. Walls upholstered in the unmistakable luxury of Fortuny fabric complete the setting.

Facing: My bathroom began with a pine fragment I found at the Paris flea market. I used it as a frame for a mirror, had a commode made to match and transformed an ordinary space into a room with warmth and a sense of history.

Above: A Biedermeier piece adds interesting contrast to an antique French mirror, a painted wooden blackamoor and an antique chemist's jar in a master bathroom.

I covered the walls with rich wood paneling in Darwin James's gentleman's bath. Antique wall sconces, an antique French mirror and a substantial commode containing a dark marble custom sink complete the masculine character of the room.

A trio of small engravings anchors an antique French barometer in a powder room.

Young girls displayed on a silver tray—one a gilded bust, the other a small painting on ivory—add to the feminine atmosphere of a lady's bath.

Just as a commode or a console can make a wonderful sink stand, a desk can take on a new function. The addition of an antique mirror and a pair of crystal lamps changed an exquisite painted desk into an even better dressing table. Lovely silk drapes frame the setting.

COCO
PARFUM
CHANEL
PARIS
Guerlain
SHALIMAR

In Linda James's bath, I converted an antique French buffet into a generous sink stand for perfumes and accessories. Antique bronze sconces light the antique trumeau mirror.

Purple hydrangeas in a soap dish add to the tropical flavor of the powder room.

Fern wallpaper in a pool house powder room introduced a botanical theme that led to fern wall sconces, botanical wall hangings, pillows and even a botanically inspired chandelier. Graphic-patterned pillows add a subtle visual link, repeating the branched lines of the ferns.

Small vanities can still accommodate pretty lighting accessories. In John and Terry Mabrey's home, a petite pair of Staffordshire lamps add finishing detail to the powder room, composed of an antique French mirror and a French commode fitted with a sink.

A grand painting of a French aristocrat dominates a powder room off of a clubroom. The custom iron base by Antique Warehouse holds a honed marble sink.

Marbles and mirrors can be beautiful, but in a bathroom too many of these cold surfaces can be too much of a good thing. To soften this area, nothing is as effective as the glow of lamplight. A custom lamp built from a French candlestick adds warmth to a large painted breakfront in a guest bath.

The hunting scene depicted in the French trumeau mirror is probably the closest thing to dirt this "mud room" will ever see. A small painted commode has become a perfect sink stand for the small space.

Earth-tone colors of "Les Veux de Paris" wallpaper by Marvic, the simple architecture of a French buffet sink base, and the restrained lines of a French Empire mirror create a pleasing atmosphere for a gentleman's bath.

varvatos

A bathroom should be functional, but there is no need to advertise it with a dreary utilitarian look. In Frank and Gayle Eby's home, we constructed the master bathroom from old French paneling and added a painted antique finish. The beautiful result offers practical convenience dressed with an elegant air.

Finding new uses for the antiques that I love let me change an ordinary space in my home into a jewel box powder room. A ho-hum bathtub and shower are thankfully out of sight behind the salvaged doors of a LXV armoire. The petite Swedish mirror is actually a mirror, but the sink is a bowl, the sink cabinet is a wonderful old Swedish stove and the tole napkin tray led a previous life as a cheese wheel.

Unlined curtains allow sunshine to stream into a master bath, a tranquil setting where wonderful "Bird and Thistle" wallpaper by Brunschwig & Fils creates a botanical backdrop for the marble tub.

A gentleman's dressing area in the country is simply accessorized with an antique Black Forest chair and a bronze deer candleholder that echo the woodland atmosphere flourishing outside the window.

An old pine chest topped with a limestone bowl adds individuality to a powder room.

A pair of trumeau mirrors (one unseen) and an antique wooden tabernacle add elegance to a guest bathroom.

I chose accessories with a bucolic flavor for the guest bath in a country home. Hand-colored bird prints, the dark wood of a Brittany box and a faux bois stone mirror all have a rural background. A small nosegay of woodland flowers adds life to the setting.

Attention to little details can transform necessities. Coordinating the color of hand towels with a rustic tray holding glass toiletries is a small touch, but it creates a pleasing repetition of color. Fresh woodland hydrangeas highlight the arrangement.

A custom jade lamp and crystal accessories highlight a vanity in a guest bathroom. "Au Pied Des Ruines" by Zoffany, a wonderful pale toile covering the dressing table chair, picks up the jade color.

The French Country Garden

In the master bedroom sitting area, vases from Linda James's extensive collection of Rose Medallion porcelain have been converted into end table lamps. The pure rose color is repeated in many of the accompanying fabrics.

There is no prettier container for flowers than a Rose Medallion porcelain vase.

A pink lustre English pitcher filled with flowers provides delightful contrast to the elegant ormolu clock on the bedside table.

Bedrooms should be restful, but they also can be interesting. I stepped outside the box a little in this master bedroom by using x-form stools covered in contemporary "Hypnotique" fabric by Calvin. Matching pillows create a relationship between very different upholstered pieces.

I don't think it's an exaggeration to say that decorating can improve the quality of your life. In this example, a good book, a graceful French fauteuil armchair and an open balcony doorway create a perfect antidote for a stressful day.

Exotic themes create a pleasing bond between the boudoir pillows and the bolster, covered in silk "Tanzania" from the Charles Faudree Collection for Vervain.

Because I used a colorful print for the pivotal fabric—"Les Pecheurs" by Brunschwig & Fils—I used muted fabrics for the bedcoverings in a guest room. The striped bed skirt is low key but adds interest to the bed linens.

A Year in the Garden
PROVENCAL

BEDSIDE PRAYERS

Previous overleaf: A quiet mix of toiles, stripes and solid-colored fabrics in silk linen and velvet are used in this luxurious master bedroom. "Folktales" toile by Fabricut covers the duvet, and "Allentown Stripe" by Fabricut covers the Directoire bergère chair.

Stacking a pair of complementary mirrors and enclosing them with a pair of antique wooden swags creates and interesting wallscape for a guest bedroom.

A pair of antique French chairs covered in "Palm Li" by Hodsoll McKenzie, separated by a French pearwood table, forms a serene seating area for a guest bedroom. For the tablescape I used a tole lamp and elevated an unusual Staffordshire white dove tureen on two white-covered books to create a focal point. The ottoman is upholstered in "Falk Manor House" by Scalamandré.

Facing: Using contrast to call attention to something is an artistic principle that has many uses in decorating. In George Fadaol's master bedroom, the shades made of antique paisley fabric are a perfect contrast to contemporary crystal lamps, highlighting the beauty of both.

Layering pillows and bed covers made of different fabrics, colors and textures creates a cozy haven in Darwin and Linda James's master bedroom. The child's upholstered chair, outfitted with a riser, is actually a dog's footstool designed by my brother-in-law, Dale Gillman. It gives Duke, the family dog, unrestricted access to his favorite spot on a fur throw.

I decorated the guest bedroom in Frank and Gayle Eby's Cashiers home with two favorite fabrics from my collection: "Hamlet's Toile" covers a pair of bergère chairs and "Biron Check" is the curtain fabric. At the time, I had no idea I also would buy a home in Cashiers or that the Ebys would designate this bedroom as my living space while my new home was being readied. Unwittingly, I was creating a nest for myself, filled with things that I love.

At times, furniture can be repurposed to do more than one job. The handsome Dutch armoire hides the television in addition to offering extra storage. The large ottoman, covered in "Preston" by Travers, has several uses: a traditional spot for propping one's feet, a spot for extra seating, or, with the addition of a tray, it becomes a nice-sized coffee table.

Oh, the mix. When it comes to fabric, I'm from the "more is better" school. I used pillows covered in a silk animal print and a silk stripe to add to the charm of a daybed upholstered in floral print "Beauclaire" from the Charles Faudree Collection for Vervain.

Getting the right color for painted walls can be tricky. For a young lady's bedroom I chose "Moss Lake" by Pratt and Lambert to create a soothing background for my pivotal fabric, "Beauclaire." A French painting that was a Paris flea market find hangs above a decorative iron bed, while a French daybed beneath the window adds an option for resting and reading.

BIRDS

The "Bird" guestroom in Frank and Gayle Eby's Carolina home takes its name from the pivotal fabric that represents a good decorating tip. I liked the fabric design a lot, but it was much too bright for the subtle look I wanted. Rather than discard the idea, I used the fabric on the reverse for a one-of-a-kind vintage look for curtains, pillows and a chair. Bird prints on the walls continue the theme, and the room is completed with a pair of custom beds.

An antique Swedish secretary harmonizes with the muted colors of a reversed fabric.

A bedroom with a nautical motif includes a custom headboard by David Hollingsworth that serves as a canvas for a painting of sailboats by artist Janet Davie and a small rug with a design of starfish and seaweed.

A pair of beds with painted headboards in a guest bedroom share a painted French writing table. Desk accessories include a deer figure, an antique pitcher holding a woodland bouquet and tole lamps, made more interesting by the addition of Lucite bases and custom lampshades of "Aiken" print fabric from the Charles Faudree Collection for Vervain.

A French Louis XV chair and ottoman covered in "Les Sylphides" by Marvic set the tone for the other soft colors and fabrics I used in Roger and Kelly Ganner's serene master bedroom. A bedside table that also functions as a desk offers a peaceful place for writing notes.

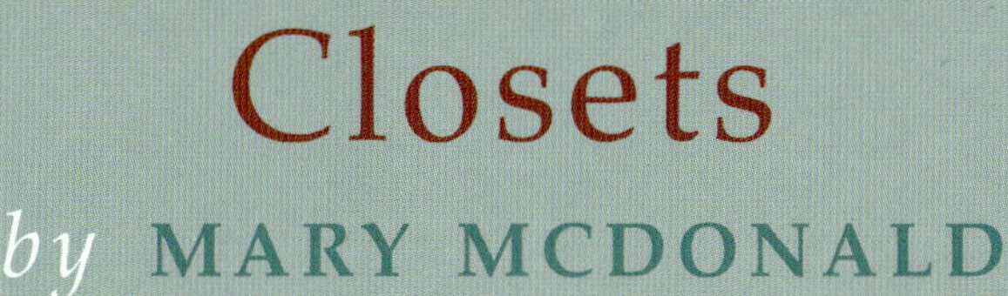

Closets

by MARY MCDONALD

I HAVE ALWAYS LOVED CLOTHES *since I was a little girl. All clothes. To me life is really just a big costume party and you never know what the theme might be next. Consequently I have had to live with tight closet space no matter what square footage I have at a given time.*

I have had numerous closets in my life in a full range of sizes. For my last closet I had the luxury of converting an office off the master bedroom. I envisioned a small salon from the days of Dior, where you could sit and lounge while you tried on shoes and jewelry and chatted on the phone a bit. It is an indulgent space, with a sofa, French chairs, ottoman and a six-foot mirrored vanity. But I find even the smallest of closets can hold a beautifully upholstered stool and a petite antique mirror. Finish with a luscious paint color and even wallpaper on the ceiling to add zip and pizazz.

Having been a milliner and accessories designer earlier in my life, I have grown accustomed to collecting an endless range of jewelry, hats, bags, scarves, silk flowers, belts and feathers. I still use all these styling accessories at one point or another to personalize my outfits. Needless to say, this is a lot of stuff to store and find in an organized manner.

I start with a list of the number of each type of clothing and accessory I have so that I know I have allocated enough drawers vs. shelves vs. containers. I include a carefully thought-out combination of both single- and double-height rods, open shelving and drawers. I use custom boxes for unruly silk flowers, feathers, paste jewelry and the like, and wall hooks (great for unused wall sections), ceiling hooks, fabric-covered accessory boxes, and doré metal towel bars for sashes and belts. I use every square inch.

I am a big believer in organizing by color. It is very helpful to organize jewelry in colored boxes: red for corals, green for jades and turquoise, and so on. When I want something blue, I hit the blue boxes. I do the same with shoes. I only arrange them by color.

Charles and I share a love of closets that are fun to be in. He has a wonderful way of displaying accessories that also provides effective storage. His use of decorative footstools adds distinction and comfort to the smallest closet. And he organizes clothing spaces beautifully.

Designers and custom closet companies offer endless closet choices, but whatever your budget I think it is important to make it personal to your style. Your closet sets the tone for you every day. Make it yours. Even a closet painted lacquer red with a small crystal fixture can evoke jewel-like glamour. Let your closet say "YOU" the instant you open the door.

Previous overleaf: I love treasure hunting for one-of-a-kind accessories, and there is no better place to hunt than in Paris. The bust of a young woman came from such a birthday shopping trip, and she has found a perfect home atop a Louis XV commode in Linda James's closet. An antique French chair and Country French gilded mirror amplify the room's Gallic theme.

Stripping away dated cabinetry and replacing it with rich paneling revived a master bedroom closet that now serves exclusively as a gentleman's closet. A gold-framed collection of letter seals complements the masculine décor.

A banquette covered in cut velvet "Cavallo" by Nancy Corzine adds seating for the gentleman's closet.

Sheryl Wagner hardware contributes to the elegance.

Space permitting, a completely equipped gentleman's closet should include a dressing counter. An antique wooden blackamoor and a pair of small lamps create an attractive tablescape for the counter shown here.

Combining freestanding pieces with built-ins can add charm and efficiency to a closet.

A Directoire armoire inspired a gentleman's closet that has been custom outfitted with paneling to match the handsome piece.

Some closets are so wonderful that instead of getting ready for a party, you feel as though you've arrived at it. A 1920s-era sleeping porch provided space for just such a dressing utopia. Moldings that are re-creations of those used in the original home, chandeliers and floor-to-ceiling mirrors form the backdrop of the exquisite conversion.

A sterling silver cake plate serves as a riser for accessories on a spacious center island.

Paneling was used to create an extensive built-in closet wardrobe.

THOMAS MORAN National Gallery of Art, Washington
DECOR The Grand Book of French Style DEMACHY and BAUDOT
BULFINCH
ALEXANDRA D'ARNOUX
JÉRÔME DARBLAY
FAMILY HOUSES by the SEA
Potter
SOURCE RECORDS of the GREAT WAR VOLUME II A.D. 1914
OKLAHOMA A Portrait of America
BRUCE CHATWIN
Frans Lanting
OKAVANGO
Ehrman and Benn
Birds and Beasts in

Collections

by RUSTY GRIMES

IT WAS THE SUMMER OF 1931, *when I was five years old. My family piled in the car in Dallas and drove to Galveston, on the Gulf Coast of Texas. It was there on the beach that I discovered I was a collector. I gathered shells and bits of shells and decorated my tent on the sand. The ocean was at my feet, but my memory is of the fun I had collecting shells.*

Since then I have collected Chinese Canton ware, English wing chairs, Toby mugs, gaudy Dutch pitchers, schoolgirl samplers, Welsh dressers and all things dog: I have English dog paintings, dog needlepoints, dog tobacco jars and dog bronzes.

In 1966 I collected my first piece of Staffordshire. It was a cow and her calf and it cost me dearly—$16 to be exact. It was also about that time that I met my good friend Charles Faudree. I taught him a few things about collecting, and he taught me how to display my collections so they are wonderful to behold and add pleasure to my life every single day.

I have added many pieces of Staffordshire to my collection and made many wonderful friends since, but I still treasure the cow and her calf, and Charles Faudree is still my best friend.

Previous overleaf: I used bookcase shelves to showcase a collection based on all things to do with the sea. Individual coral and shell specimens were made much more interesting by expanding the collection to include shell topiaries, a framed French collage of shells centered with a medallion, and a seashell painting by Jimmy Steinmeyer.

An unusual painted French cupboard is a color-coordinated platform for a collection of celadon vases centered between antique alter sticks. A second collection, composed of antique pillows decorating a daybed, is an example of the variety of interesting things that can be collected.

Accessorizing Bob and Ann Osborne's Texas home involved a lot more sorting than shopping. Ann is a wonderful collector and her many interests translate into a variety of marvelous objects for decorating walls and tables. In the clubroom, her Faience collection predominates. Faience plates flank a painting and Faience vases highlight the French stone mantel. Completing the room's décor, Alex, a highly decorative Westie, perches on a Country French chair upholstered in "Plougastel" by Brunschwig and Fils.

A collection of antique Palissy and majolica plates are mixed with antique books on the shelves of a French buffet de corps. *A wonderful Palissy plate is even better when you think outside the box: I didn't have a plate stand but did have a nice wooden easel that is used to elevate and display things. Wiring the plate to its impromptu stand created an unexpected and eye-catching presentation that makes the whole collection more enjoyable.*

Empress Eugénie, Napoleon III's wife, was an early collector of art glass paperweights that originated in France in the mid-1800s. Showcased on a book top, a colorful paperweight collection makes a pleasing accessory.

When I gave Bill Carpenter a poodle dog match striker, I should have known that one piece would trigger the start of a wonderful collection. Bill is a dog person too and collects "anything dog." His striker collection has many dog figures, but he also has included other interesting finds, including his favorite—a match striker of the Queen's Hamlet at Versailles. On covered match strikers, the striker is on the underside of the lid.

Facing: Large collections can be used to create wonderful wallscapes. A small French cabinet is laden with antique majolica oyster and asparagus plates and is flanked by a symmetrical arrangement from the remainder of the collection.

A small collection made up of three santos *figures From Mexico and Spain embellish an antique French commode. My rule of thumb for deciding whether something is a collection is simple: one is good, two are usually a pair and three are definitely a collection.*

George Fadaol's Staffordshire dogs hold court in this charming living room tablescape.

An impressive example of Linda James's numerous equestrian trophies is a featured accessory in her office.

I love using my clients' collections to create interesting personal wallscapes. Part of the Mabreys' large collection of Flow Blue transferware—named for the blurred glaze developed for earthenware in the 1800s—surrounds a 19th-century Chinese jar on a Louis XVI–style bracket.

Collections can be especially pleasing when they complement the fabrics in a room. A Palissy majolica plate on a bracket surrounded by majolica oyster plates echoes the colors of the pillow fabrics. The oyster plates also reflect the seaside setting of this Cape Cod home.

Layering a variety of Imari and oxblood porcelains from Ann Osborne's marvelous collection of Oriental art magnifies the interest of each piece. Vases, plates and platters from different dynasties are hung and displayed on rosewood stands to create individual vignettes on each shelf.

In their Carolina home, a tabletop holds a photograph of Frank and Gayle Eby's dog, Lulu, and a tray filled with Gayle's wonderful collection of Mauchline Ware boxes. The Scottish souvenir boxes, made of pale-grained sycamore and decorated with scenes or tartans, were early Victorian collectibles.

I lined a Country French buffet with a small checked fabric to create an interesting background for a collection of Imari porcelain.

Collections can fill many rooms or begin with a single piece. A rare cave à liqueur *camel is a striking first object for a collection.*

The discovery of a second unique cave à liqueur, *this one featuring an elephant, adds to a collection.*

Guerlain flacons, *or bottles, were first made in 1828 as containers for Eau de Cologne Impériale for Empress Eugénie. The bottles are fun to collect and make a handsome addition to my bathroom.*

As you can see from this small sample, I am a compulsive bow-tie collector. Even if I wore ties every day, I couldn't wear them all, and at this point I'm not sure where they all came from. Many are gifts, but I must confess that I still keep buying more for myself, too. I just love looking at them.

My slippers are a way I pamper myself and so, naturally, they have become a collection.

Traveling and collecting are natural companions. You will learn more about the places you visit, meet interesting people and, with any luck, bring home a treasure that will always remind you of a special trip. In addition to being beautiful, Carol Bump's collection of tortoiseshell holds happy memories of trips to England and France. Centering a lone silver box and stacking a tiny tortoiseshell box on top creates a focal point for the display.

Since I love everything to do with dogs, it probably comes as no surprise that a table filled with dog figures of all kinds is a cherished collection. This photograph appeared in one of my early books, but I treasure it and wanted to share it again.

I started my collection of white Staffordshire cows over forty years ago. I've moved on to collect other things now, but I still have this collection and it is one of my favorites. Staffordshire figures are the most available of all Victorian pottery and are a great choice for starting a collection.

Barbotine plates—named for a technique of pottery styling usually featuring raised flowers or fruit—make an effective dining room wall display.

Resources

CALIFORNIA

Ann Dennis
2915 Red Hill Avenue, Suite B106
Costa Mesa, CA 92626
714.708.2555
www.anndennisdesigns.net

Hollyhock
927 North La Cienega Boulevard
Los Angeles, CA 90069
310.777.0100
www.hollyhock.net

Terra Cotta
11922 San Vicente Boulevard
Los Angeles, CA 90046
310.826.7878

Villa Melrose
6061 West 3rd Street
Los Angeles, CA 90036
323.934.8130
www.villamelroseantiques.com

Jeffries Ltd
852 Production Place
Newport Beach, CA 92663
949.642.4154
www.jefferiesltd.com

Tom Stansbury Antiques
466 Old Newport Boulevard
Newport Beach, CA 92663
949.642.1272
www.tomstandburyantiques.com

Lief
646 North Almont Drive
West Hollywood, CA 90069
310.492.0033
www.liefaa.com

COLORADO

Gorsuch, Ltd.
138 Beaver Creek Plaza
Avon, CO 81620
970.949.7115
www.gorsuch.com

263 East Gore Creek Drive
Vail, CO 81657
970.476.2294
www.gorsuch.com

The Shaggy Ram
210 Edwards Village Boulevard
A-209
Edwards, CO 81632
970.926.7377
www.theshaggyram.com

NEW YORK

John Derian
6 East Second Street
New York City, NY 10003
212.677.3917
www.johnderian.com

John Rosselli
523 East 73rd Street
New York City, NY 10021
212.772.2137
www.johnrosselliantiques.com

Royal Antiques
60 East 11th Street, Suite #1
New York City, NY 10003
212.533.6390

Treillage Ltd.
418 East 75th Street
New York City, NY 10021
212.535.2288
www.bunnywilliams.com/treillage

NORTH CAROLINA

Village Antiques
755 Biltmore Avenue
Asheville, NC 28803
828.252.5090
www.villageantiquesonline.com

Dovetail Antiques
252 Highway 107 South
Cashiers, NC 28717
818.743.1800

Francie Hargrove
25 Burn Street
Cashiers, NC 28717
478.756.8088
www.franciehargrove.com

Rusticks
32 Canoe Point
Cashiers, NC 28717
828.743.3172
www.rusticks.com

Ryan & Company
551 Highway 107 South
Cashiers, NC 28717
828.743.6767

Vivianne Metzger Antiques
31 Canoe Point
Cashiers, NC 28717
828.743.0642
www.vmantiques.com

Neal Johnson Ltd.
601 South Cedar Street, Suite 205B
Charlotte, NC 28202
704.377.1099
www.nealjohnsonltd.com

Acorn's Boutique
465 Main Street
Highlands, NC 28741
828.787.2640

C K Swan & Harlee Gallery
233 North 4th Street
Highlands, NC 28741
828.526.2083
www.ckswan.com

A Country Home
5162 US Highway 64 East
Highlands, NC 28741
828.526.9038

Nest
802 North 4th Street
Highlands, NC 28741
828.526.5023
Www.nesthighlands.com

Thomas Hoke Antiques Warehouse
125 Lane Parkway
Salisbury, NC 28146
704.467.3456
www.thomashokeantiques.com

OKLAHOMA

Bebe's
6480 Avondale Drive
Oklahoma City, OK 73116
405.843.8431
www.shopbebes.com

Covington Antiques
7100 North Western Avenue
Oklahoma City, OK 73116
405.842.3030

The Antiquary
1325 East 15th Street
Tulsa, OK 74120
918.582.2897

Antique Warehouse, Dale Gillman
2406 East 12th Street
Tulsa, OK 74104
918.592.2900

Embellishments
1345 East 15th Street
Tulsa, OK 74120
918.585.8688

Leslie Elliott Interiors
9130 South Sheridan Road
Tulsa, OK 74133
918.622.6562
www.leslieelliottinteriors.com

Polo Lodge Antiques
8250 East 41st Street
Tulsa, OK 74145
918.622.3227

Royce Meyers Art, Ltd.
1706 South Boston
Tulsa, OK 74119
918.582.0288
www.roycemeyers.com

T. A. Lorton
1343 East 15th Street
Tulsa, OK 74120
918.743.1600
www.talorton.com

Toni's Flowers
3549 South Harvard Avenue
Tulsa, OK 74135
918.742.9027
www.tonisflowersgifts.com

TENNESSEE

Catherine Harris
2215 Merchants Row, Suite 1
Germantown, TN 38138
901.753.0999

French Country Imports
6225 Poplar Pike
Memphis, TN 38119
901.682.2000
www.frenchcountryimports.com

Jimmy Graham Interiors
3092 Poplar Avenue Suite # 17
Memphis, TN 38111
901.323.2322

La Maison Antiques, LLC
4768 Poplar Avenue
Memphis, TN 38117
901.537.0009
www.lamaisonantiques.com

Market Central
2215 Central Avenue
Memphis, TN 38104
901.276.3809

The Palladio Market
2169 Central Avenue
Memphis, TN 38104
901.276.3808
www.thepalladiomarket.com

TEXAS

Country French Antiques
1428 Slocum Street
Dallas, TX 75207
215.747.4700

The Gathering Galleries
955 Slocum Street
Dallas, TX 75207
214.741.4888

Inessa Stewart's Antiques
5201 West Lovers Lane
Dallas, Texas 75209
214.366.2660
www.inessa.com

1643 Dragon Street
Dallas, TX 75207
214.742.5800
www.inessa.com

Joseph Minton Antiques
1410 Slocum Street
Dallas, TX 75207
214.744.3111
Mintonantiques.com

The Mews
1708 Market Center Boulevard
Dallas, TX 75207
214.748.9070

Nick Brock Antiques
2909 North Henderson Avenue
Dallas, TX 75206
214.828.0624
www.nickbrockantiques.com

Uncommon Market
100 Riveredge Drive
Dallas, TX 75207
214.871.2775
www.uncommonmarketinc.com

The Whimsey Shoppe
1444 Oak Lawn Avenue, Suite 215
Dallas, TX 75207
214.745.1800
www.thewhimseyshoppe.com

Chateau Domingue
3615-B West Alabama Street
Houston, TX 77027
713.961.3444
www.chateaudomingue.com

Gray Door
3465 West Alabama, Suite A
Houston, TX 77027
713.521.9085
www.graydoorantiques.com

Joyce Horn Antiques, Ltd.
1022 Wirt Road, Suite 326
Houston, TX 77055
713.688.0507
www.joycehornantiques.com

Kay O'Toole Antiques & Eccentricities
1921 Westheimer Road
Houston, TX 77098
713.523.1921
www.kayotooleantiques.com

Neal and Company Antiques
4502 Greenbriar Street
Houston, TX 77005
713.942.9800

Watkins Culver Antiques
2308 Bissonnet Street
Houston, TX 77005
713.529.0597
www.watkinsculverantiques.com

White & Day Antiques
6711 F.M. 1960 Road West
Houston, TX 77069
281.444.3836

Acknowledgments

People ask if I get tired of writing books because it must be so lonely. I am happy to say it's just the opposite: not only am I surrounded by a mob of people, they are some of my best friends. This book is actually written with their help. It passes along many of their ideas and owes much to their inspiration. I am in the lucky center of a busy, entertaining (at times hilarious) creative process that includes my clients, staff, editor, writer, photographer and family. I cherish them all.

First, I want to thank Francesanne Tucker for spending so many hours with me, pushing me to make deadlines and making my half-sentences coherent. She is my dear friend, wonderful and witty and smart. We had many laughs and good times.

My thanks, again, to Jenifer Jordan for her beautiful pictures. We, too, had many a good time and plenty of laughs.

I am always grateful to Toni Garner. She does all the beautiful flowers in this book. I love her dearly.

All my gratitude and love to the following talented friends who authored the introductions to each section of this book, adding their wealth of expertise and their unique creative insights: Hal Ainsworth, Barry Dixon, David Easton, Gayle Eby, Francie Faudree, Rusty Grimes, Linda James, Mary McDonald, Lisa Newsom, Winton Noah, and James Steinmeyer.

I know this book would not have come about, nor the rooms have been finished, without my amazing staff. Kudos to Megan Phillips, Darcie Blackerby, John Wilferth, Polly Batchelor, Bill Carpenter, George Fadaol and Kyle Hatfield. Also thanks to all the people in my work rooms that make me look good.

I especially would like to thank the following homeowners (and friends) for allowing me to help in the decoration of their homes and for agreeing to share their rooms in this book: Steve and Gayle Allen, Jeff and Sheryl Bashaw, Stewart and Kate Beal, George Fadaol, David and Cindy Foster, Larry and Carol Bump, Bill Carpenter, Susie Collins, Frank and Gayle Eby, Roger and Kelly Ganner, Gary and Donna Gilliam, Darwin and Linda James, John and Julie Nickel, John and Terry Mabrey, Bob and Ann Osborne, Jeffery and Lisa Rowsey, Steven and Gaye Sherman, Mark and Cassie Shires, James and Julie Welch and the Women of Kappa Alpha Theta.

Many thanks to Madge Baird, my editor and dear friend, for her commitment and guidance. I have the greatest respect for her.

My family is forever important for helping me maintain a crazy schedule while keeping my sense of humor, my perspective and my sanity. My deepest thanks and all my love to my sister and my partner, Francie Faudree and Bill Carpenter; my brother-in-law Dale Gillman; and my precious Cavalier Spaniels, Ruby and Lila.

Finally, to all of you, my deepest gratitude for allowing me to share my love of decorating, furnishing, fabrics, and, of course, my love of all dogs, decorative or not. I hope this book gives you new ideas to use in your own homes.

Merci beaucoup,
Charles Faudree